I0453886

A NEW LIFE IN CHRIST

Becoming Established in
Your Newly Found Faith

Terry L. Young

Unless otherwise indicated, all Scripture quotations in this volume are taken from the *New King James Version®*. Copyright © 1982 by Thomas Nelson. Used by permission. All rights reserved.

Scripture quotations marked (*KJV*) are taken from the King James Version of the Bible. Public domain.

Scripture quotations marked (*NIV*) are taken from the Holy Bible, New International Version®, NIV®. Copyright © 1973, 1978, 1984, 2011 by Biblica, Inc.™ Used by permission of Zondervan. All rights reserved worldwide. www.zondervan.com The "NIV" and "New International Version" are trademarks registered in the United States Patent and Trademark Office by Biblica, Inc.™

A New Life in Christ:
Becoming Established in Your Newly Found Faith

ISBN # 979-8-218-16514-7
Copyright © 2023 by Terry L. Young
T-N-T Ministries International
P.O. Box 712
Morgantown, WV 26507 USA
Published by Terry L. Young
www.tntmissions.org

Text Design: Lisa Simpson
Cover Design: Emanuel Kasemi

Printed in the United States of America. All rights reserved under International Copyright Law. No portion of this book may be reproduced or transmitted in any form or by any means — electronic, mechanical, photocopy, recording, scanning, or other — except for brief quotations in critical reviews or articles, without the prior written permission of the Publisher.

Italicized portions of Bible verses indicate the author's emphasis.

~❧

Jesus answered and said to him,
"Most assuredly, I say to you, unless one is born again,
he cannot see the kingdom of God."

John 3:3

CONTENTS

PREFACE

As we move closer to the day of Christ's return, many are moving further away from God's Word — and they don't even realize it. In the Church, this move is incremental; in society, it has become a paradigm shift.

Society, as a whole, has now thrown off the eternal, immutable (unchanging) truths of what God says in His Word, the Bible, and has embraced man's philosophy of self as the highest form of truth.

Slowly following that trend, many churches that do not embrace God's Word as their final authority have allowed the world's philosophy to creep into their pulpits, and the minds of those listening have been affected by the world without knowing it.

God is clear in telling us that His Word is final and eternal, to which we are accountable.

In this book, I want to instruct those seeking to know God better in a clear, truthful, and simple way. We must approach God on *His* terms. There is no other way. God created you, this world, the universe, and all that is in them. If we are to know Him, we must know Him through His pathway — Jesus Christ.

Jesus will soon return for His people. After that, it will be too late. We must act now.

INTRODUCTION

ALL OF US ARE BORN with sinful hearts. We are born not as pure, innocent babies but with an inward nature that is selfish, evil, and rebellious. This *sinful nature* is a consequence of the first man and woman's disobedience to God, and it is within every one of us. We inherited this sinful nature from the first man and woman, Adam and Eve.

Due to this inherent, sinful nature, a great wall of separation arose between humanity and God. Our relationship and communication with the God who created us were utterly destroyed.

There is only one way for you and me to regain what was lost when mankind sinned. We can enter once again into a relationship with God only by what Jesus called being "born again."

We must first be cleansed from our sinfulness and given a new nature in God. The only way for this cleansing to happen is through the Blood of Jesus, whom God punished for our sins.

The New Birth, or being "born again," as the Bible calls it, is the most crucial decision in a person's life. Where we spend eternity is at stake!

Who do we believe Jesus Christ is? Have we been changed or transformed from being a sinner into a born-again believer?

1

**The New Birth, or being "born again,"
as the Bible calls it, is the most crucial decision
in a person's life.**

Our answers to those questions determine whether we will spend eternity in Heaven with God, or in the eternal torment of a literal, fiery hell and ultimately in the "…lake which burns with fire and brimstone, which is the second death" (Revelation 21:8).

Your answers to those questions will determine where *you* will spend eternity.

This book will explain what it means to be born again, how to become a new creation in Christ, and what the result of being born again should be. We need to know how to develop and maintain an authentic relationship with God by living according to God's Word.

The New Testament clearly teaches that man cannot become righteous independently, in and of our own power. It takes God's Spirit to regenerate the human spirit.

In addition, no one can live a godly life until God actually enables that person to do so. For that to happen, we must accept the Lordship of Jesus Christ, allowing the Spirit of God to cleanse us from sin and change our sinful nature. Jesus said, "…you must be born again."

Jesus said, "…you must be born again."

Chapter 1

You Must Be Born Again

D URING JESUS' MINISTRY ON THE earth, He did many miraculous things that gave evidence that God sent Him. It was evident to everyone in Israel that He was a teacher who came from God.

A man came to Jesus, who was a "ruler of the Jews" (John 3:1). This man's name was Nicodemus.

As a leader of the Jews, Nicodemus was obviously a very religious and educated person. He was impressed with the ministry of Jesus and was touched by the fact that Jesus had the blessing of God. He came to Jesus by night and said, "Rabbi, we know that thou art a teacher come from God: for no man can do these miracles that thou doest, except God be with him" (John 3:2 *KJV*).

It was obvious to Nicodemus that Jesus was not an ordinary rabbi. Jesus had power from God. That power and authority captured Nicodemus's attention, as the man was a believer in the law of Moses and the writings of the Old Testament prophets.

As Jesus often did when he spoke with religious people, he said something that shook Nicodemus's theology.

Jesus spoke about a *difficult spiritual truth* for this man to grasp.

When Nicodemus observed God was with Jesus because of the works He did, Jesus responded, "Most assuredly, I say to you, unless one is born again, he cannot see the kingdom of God" (John 3:3).

This very spiritual truth was difficult for Nicodemus to grasp. Although he was sincere, as evidenced by his coming to Jesus to find the truth about eternal life, he could not learn eternal truths simply with his intellect.

Nicodemus was a man who followed the law of Moses. He was accustomed to doing acts of good works to gain favor with God by obligation. So, when Jesus presented a spiritual truth that dealt with the inner man, Nicodemus could not comprehend it.

In verse 4 of this passage, Nicodemus was incredulous and exclaimed, "How can a man be born when he is old? Can he enter a second time into his mother's womb, and be born?" (John 3:4). His question came from a natural point of view rather than from any spiritual insight.

The trouble with people is that they see things through the physical senses only. Man's spiritual understanding is darkened because of the sinful nature within him.

God Looks at the Inner Man

For example, in the Old Testament, we see the account of the prophet Samuel going to Bethlehem to anoint a new king for Israel. God had already rejected Saul (the first king of Israel) for his repeated disobedience to God's commandments.

In First Samuel 15:11, we read that God told Samuel, "I greatly regret that I have set up Saul as king, for he has turned back from following Me, and has not performed My commandments."

The Lord then told the prophet Samuel to go to the town of Bethlehem to the house of a man named Jesse. The Lord said, "I am sending you to Jesse the Bethlehemite. For I have provided Myself a king among his sons" (1 Samuel 16:1).

When Samuel came to Jesse's house, he told Jesse that he had come to sacrifice unto the Lord. "Then he consecrated Jesse and his sons, and invited them to the sacrifice" (1 Samuel 16:5).

When the sons of Jesse came before Samuel, the Bible says he "looked at Eliab" (1 Samuel 16:6) and thought that he was surely the anointed one for whom the Lord had sent him.

Eliab was David's oldest brother and was a seasoned warrior. He must have looked magnificent, for even the prophet of God thought he must be the one whom God would call to be the new king of Israel.

Saul, the first king, was a magnificent-looking man. When he was chosen to be king, the Bible says that Saul was "a choice and handsome son whose name was Saul. There was

5

not a more handsome person than he among the children of Israel. From his shoulders upward he was taller than any of the people" (1 Samuel 9:2).

Perhaps Samuel the prophet remembered the appearance of the first king and assumed that God would choose such a man to replace him.

Nevertheless, the Lord told Samuel, "But the LORD said to Samuel, 'Do not look at his appearance or at his physical stature, because I have refused him. For the LORD does not see as man sees; for man looks at the outward appearance, but *the LORD looks at the heart*'" (1 Samuel 16:7).

The very core of the problem between God and man is the heart!

For the Lord does not see as man sees;
for man looks at the outward appearance,
but the Lord looks at the heart.
1 Samuel 16:7

While we tend to look at outward appearance, while God looks inside a man and sees what he is. Nothing is hidden from Him.

'Whitewashed Tombs'

On one particular occasion, Jesus confronted the Pharisees for their hypocrisy by saying:

"Woe to you, scribes and Pharisees, hypocrites! For you are like whitewashed tombs which indeed appear beautiful outwardly, but inside are full of dead men's bones and all uncleanness. Even so, you also *outwardly appear righteous* to men, but *inside you are full of hypocrisy and lawlessness.*"

Matthew 23:27–28

This analogy Jesus uses to refer to the most religious people of His day was striking! The Pharisees were the most orthodox of the Jews, who endeavored to fulfill every letter of the law of Moses and all the writings of the rabbis.

They observed the Law to the *nth* degree, but they also made a show of it openly so they could have the praise of men and the status of being perceived as righteous. They went to great lengths, even extreme measures, to appear righteous through their religious works to obtain political power and status. They wielded power and authority, punishing those they determined to be lawbreakers while being wicked themselves.

Here, in Matthew's gospel, Jesus points out their hypocrisy and uncleanness by saying they appeared pure and holy on the exterior. Yet inside, they were filled with cruelty and callousness, or as Jesus said, "…but inside you are full of hypocrisy and lawlessness" (Matthew 23:28).

We see this same illustration used by the Apostle Paul when he stood trial before the chief priest and the high priests who were trying to condemn him.

Then Paul, looking earnestly at the council, said, "Men and brethren, I have lived in all good conscience

before God until this day." And the high priest Ananias commanded those who stood by him to strike him on the mouth. Then Paul said to him, "God will strike you, you *whitewashed wall*! For you sit to judge me according to the Law, and do you command me to be struck contrary to the Law?"

Acts 23:1–3

The same idea of hypocrisy is brought forth in this passage. The council looked good and religious on the outside; however, they failed to follow the Law and righteousness inside.

The prophet Hosea wrote, "For I desire mercy and not sacrifice, and the knowledge of God more than burnt offerings. But like men, they transgressed the covenant; there they dealt treacherously with Me" (Hosea 6:6–7).

Therefore, the issue that Jesus dealt with when Nicodemus asked Him about eternal life was the need for cleansing from this inner wickedness.

Man needed a spiritual answer to a spiritual problem. Religious works will never be enough to bring about an actual change inside of us. Religion can act as a salve, soothing our souls into a false sense of well-being. In and of themselves, righteous works do not produce the right relationship with God that mankind is seeking.

In and of themselves, righteous works
do not produce the right relationship with God
that mankind is seeking.

The reason that works will never be enough is a result of the fact that man is sinful inside. Man's character and very nature is sinful. No matter how many religious works man does, it comes from a sinful, fallen nature. Religious works are like that "whitewashed wall" Paul wrote about or the "whitewashed tombs" Jesus spoke about. All of it is hypocrisy.

CHAPTER 2

AN INWARD CHANGE MUST TAKE PLACE

Jesus answered Nicodemus's question about a man being born when he is old by saying, "Most assuredly, I say to you, unless one is born of water and the Spirit, he cannot enter the kingdom of God. That which is born of the flesh is flesh, and that which is born of the Spirit is spirit" (John 3:5–6).

"Most assuredly, I say to you, unless one is born of water and the Spirit, he cannot enter the kingdom of God."
John 3:5

To simplify that statement with more modern language, Jesus said there is a difference between our inner person and fleshly, external bodies. He said:

"Flesh gives birth to flesh, but the Spirit gives birth to spirit."

John 3:6 (*NIV*)

Unless a person is changed by the Spirit of God (born of the water and of the Spirit), he *cannot* enter God's Kingdom. There must be a change in our *spirit man*.

Our spirit is the eternal part of us. Unless our spirit is born "of the Spirit," we cannot enter the kingdom of God. Without that spiritual change, we remain sinful, retaining the sinful nature we inherited from Adam and Eve. Sin cannot stand in the presence of a holy God.

We must also understand that individual *acts of sin* are not the issue with God regarding our salvation. The question Jesus addresses here is not how many particular big or little sins we have committed. The more significant issue is the *sinful nature* of mankind.

We *are* sinners. We commit individual sins because it is in our very nature to do so. Committing a sin, in and of itself, does not make us a sinner. We sin because of who we are already.

It's just like an old rooster. A rooster crows because it is a rooster. Crowing day and night is what it does because it is what it is, a rooster. A dog barks because it is a dog. A duck quacks because it is a duck. It is their nature to do so.

The fact that man is sinful is well established throughout history and well documented in the Bible. God's Word says, "For all have sinned and fall short of the glory of God" (Romans 3:23).

In the book of Galatians, Paul writes, "But the *Scripture hath concluded all under sin*, that the promise by faith of Jesus Christ might be given to them that believe" (Galatians 3:22 *KJV*). God is very clear on this subject. *All* of us have sinned against God.

For all have sinned and fall short of the glory of God.
Romans 3:23

The Apostle John wrote, "If we say that we have no sin, we deceive ourselves, and the truth is not in us" (1 John 1:8).

Most people alive today and, indeed, the majority who ever lived have rejected the truth of God's Word. They have deceived themselves into thinking they are either without sin or they are somehow good enough to stand in God's presence based on their own merits or goodness.

They say, "I don't need God! Religion is just a crutch for weak people." Karl Marx infamously said, "Religion is the opiate of the people."

However, when God spoke through the prophet Isaiah, He said, "All we like sheep have gone astray; we have turned, every one, to his own way; and the Lord has laid on Him the iniquity of us all" (Isaiah 53:6).

We have all "gone astray." We have all wandered off from God and turned to our own way of doing things. We became autonomous from God.

A prominent facet of the fallen nature of man is the arrogance of thinking either that we are without inherent sinfulness or that we are good enough to satisfy God without turning from sin.

However, the Scriptures unambiguously tell us, "All unrighteousness is sin…" (1 John 5:17).

There would have been no need for Jesus to come into the world, live a sinless life, die on the Cross, and suffer the judgment and wrath of God for our sins if we could have cleansed ourselves without His sacrifice. Further still, if we did not need forgiveness and the blotting out of our sins, Jesus would not have died for us. He would not have needed to. But we were hopelessly lost in sin because of our very spiritual nature to sin. Sinful rebellion against God and God's truth is the first sign or evidence of this nature.

But thank God, there is hope! The last part of this verse in Isaiah 53:6 says, "…the Lord has laid on Him the iniquity of us all." Jesus Christ became our substitute. He was punished for our sins.

As a result, mankind can finally be changed inside and become a new creation in Christ.

Therefore, if anyone is in Christ, he is a new creation; old things have passed away; behold, all things have become new.

2 Corinthians 5:17

This new creation, this new man, is the miraculous result of the finished work of Christ. It is not merely a religious work or an affiliation with a "religion." This new creation is what Jesus was explaining to Nicodemus, that a man's spirit could be born of God. We can become a new person, alive unto God.

This new creation is something that reaches the very core of our humanity. We are changed! "Old things have passed away; behold, all things have become new" (2 Corinthians 5:17). This is something that religion can never offer.

Paul wrote that our salvation comes "not by works of righteousness which we have done, but according to His mercy He saved us, through the washing of regeneration and renewing of the Holy Spirit" (Titus 3:5).

However, it is utterly sad that many so-called "Christian" churches and all world religions we see today teach a false doctrine. That false doctrine teaches that we must do works (perform actions or religious duty in our own human ability) to get to heaven and strive to achieve righteousness (right-relationship with God) through vain religion.

We can never achieve that, however, and that is why Jesus told Nicodemus, "Do not marvel that I said to you, 'You must be born again'" (John 3:7). We *must* be changed; we must become a new creation (a new person) in Christ.

> **"Do not marvel that I said to you,**
> **'You must be born again.'"**
> **John 3:7**

15

CHAPTER 3

HOW TO BECOME A GENUINE, BORN-AGAIN CHRISTIAN

WE HAVE ALREADY READ JESUS' emphatic statement that "...*unless one is born again*, he cannot see the kingdom of God" (John 3:3).

This leaves no room for any alternative. Jesus Christ, the Son of God, said it, and that settles it. He is the final authority on the subject.

Two Important Prerequisites

You must recognize two critical things before you can even become a child of God. If you meet these two requirements, you are a candidate to become a true Christian. Once you have settled these two facts in your heart and mind, you can then act on what you believe.

Number One:
Recognize the fact that you are a sinner.

As we have already seen, God's Word tells us that we have broken God's Law and are sinful by nature.

We must open our hearts and be honest with ourselves concerning this matter. Our sinfulness is something that we must openly acknowledge and confess to God.

Number Two:
Accept the fact that
Christ died to save you from your sins.

To be more fully convinced of this point, we must look at what the Scriptures tell us. We will look at this truth more fully here since we already covered the sin question in the previous chapter.

---

*Christ died to save you
from your sins.*

Christ Died to Save Us

Even before the time of Christ, God's prophets proclaimed His coming and what the results of His suffering would bring. In the book of Isaiah, we see that He took our sins. Speaking of Jesus, Isaiah writes,

> **Therefore I will divide Him a portion with the great, and He shall divide the spoil with the strong, because *He poured out His soul unto death,* and He was numbered**

with the transgressors, and *He bore the sin* of many, and made intercession for the transgressors.

Isaiah 53:12

Isaiah is often considered a significant Old Testament prophet because he wrote more about our redemption in Christ than any other prophet. Christ's death, burial, and resurrection fulfilled what Isaiah had written more than 700 years before those events occurred.

After the resurrection of Christ from the dead, God explained more fully what happened by inspiring the Apostle Paul to write, "For when we were still without strength, in due time Christ died for the ungodly" (Romans 5:6).

And, "For to this end Christ died and rose and lived again, that He might be Lord of both the dead and the living" (Romans 14:9).

Further, in the letters to the church in the city of Corinth, Paul wrote, "For I delivered to you first of all that which I also received: that *Christ died for our sins according to the Scriptures*" (1 Corinthians 15:3).

The Apostle Paul wrote over half of the New Testament. His revelation of what Christ did is the most important information we have about the death, burial, resurrection, and even the present-day ministry of Jesus Christ.

He also wrote, "...*He died for all*, that those who live should live no longer for themselves, but for Him who died for them and rose again" (2 Corinthians 5:15).

These and many other Scriptures tell us how important it was for Jesus to die for our sins. In fact, the reason Christ had to die was to satisfy justice. Jesus took our place; He became our substitute.

In Second Corinthians 5:19 Paul explained, "…that God was in Christ reconciling the world to himself, not imputing their trespasses to them…." He continued, "For *He made Him who knew no sin to be sin for us,* that we might become the righteousness of God in Him" (2 Corinthians 5:21).

> ***Jesus took our place;***
> ***He became our substitute.***

Jesus did not deserve to die and take our sins; He was the only person who ever fulfilled the Law of Moses without breaking any of them. He lived a sinless life and did not deserve punishment. However, to be punished for our sins is the very reason He came in the first place. His sinless life qualified Jesus to become our substitute.

God loved everyone in the world so much that He "…was in Christ *reconciling* the world to himself, *not imputing* their trespasses to them…" (2 Corinthians 5:19). That means God is not counting up or "imputing" our sins against us; instead, He is inviting us to enter a restored relationship with Himself.

According to W.E. Vine's *Dictionary of New Testament Words*, the word "reconcile" means that God exercised His grace toward sinful man based on the death of Christ, whom God judged according to *our* sins. (*See* studybible.info/vines.)

God is offering a change in relationship between Himself and humanity. We can now change from being an enemy of God to being a friend of God.

Even though we were alienated from God, He now invites us to be reconciled to Himself. That means we are asked to change our attitude toward God and reunite with Him in a restored relationship.

For if when we were enemies we were reconciled to God through the death of His Son, much more, having been reconciled, we shall be saved by His life.

Romans 5:10

This is the same word used before — *"reconciled."* To quote W.E. Vine's again, "...that we were 'enemies' not only expresses man's hostile attitude to God but signifies that until this change of attitude takes place, men are under condemnation, exposed to God's wrath." (*See* studybible.info/vines.)

Therefore, we recognize, admit, and confess that we are sinners and that Christ died for our sins. As we acknowledge and believe, there are two and only two things we must do to be saved.

I say *must do* because you will not be changed in your spirit man and become a born-again person without doing these two things.

Let me show you the important words of Paul that tell us what must be done.

That if you *confess* with your mouth the Lord Jesus and *believe* in your heart that God has raised Him from the dead, you will be saved. For with the heart one believes

unto righteousness, and with the mouth confession is made unto salvation.

Romans 10:9–10

According to this Scripture, we must *confess* and *believe* to be saved, or "born again." Let's discuss both of those actions of our faith.

Repent and Confess Him as Your Lord

The first thing we see in this Scripture is that "if you *confess* with your mouth the Lord Jesus..." (Romans 10:9).

First, there *must be* the confession of sin and true repentance.

The Bible teaches that men *must repent* to be saved. It is not enough to repeat a prayer and simply say that Jesus is your Lord if you do not repent from the sin that separated you from God in the first place.

It would be untrue to claim that the Lord Jesus is your master and Lord if you esteem sin in your heart and intend to keep any form of sin in your heart. If you're saving it up for later use, then Jesus isn't your Lord at all. Let us be honest about this: Our eternal destiny is at stake!

Confessing Jesus as Lord, by its very definition, means repenting from sin, Satan, and our old nature!

Sadly, many people attending our modern-day churches think they are "saved," yet they have never really been *changed*. They have become religious, perhaps, but they are not bearing the "fruits worthy of repentance" (Matthew 3:8). That means they are not producing a corresponding lifestyle with their profession of a true relationship with the Lord. They are not acting like Christians because they cannot be something they are not.

Confessing Jesus as Lord, by its very definition, means repenting from sin, Satan, and our old nature!

Jesus spoke quite often of fruit. He said we would know whether a tree was good or bad by the tree's fruit. He compared that directly to people. We will know them by their fruit (*see* Matthew 7:17–20).

Therefore, it is insufficient to claim Jesus as our Lord if we are unwilling to repent or turn away from and forsake our sinful nature, renouncing it altogether. Glibly saying a trite little "prayer" without meaning what we say is dangerous and self-deceptive.

What Does It Mean to Repent?

True repentance consists of several factors. The very foundational element is a sense of personal guilt and remorse. If we do not feel personally guilty for our sins, we are not ready to be forgiven for them.

For example, David, the king of Israel, once made a series of mistakes, trying to cover them as he went along. His cover-up led him into a series of compounded sins, worsening as he spiraled out of control. The mighty man of God and king of Israel had become an adulterous, murdering, corrupt liar.

The prophet of God exposed his many sins. When the prophet Nathan confronted David, he began to cry out for mercy from God. King David acknowledged his sins and asked God to wash him and purge him of every evil in his heart. He strongly felt his own sinfulness when he said, "Against You, You only, have I sinned, and done this evil in your sight… Behold, I was brought forth in iniquity, and in sin my mother conceived me" (Psalm 51:4–5).

David went on to say, "Create in me a clean heart, O God, and renew a steadfast spirit within me" (Psalm 51:10).

His deepest desire was to become clean and right before God, and he felt genuine sorrow for his sin. Yet this kind of sorrow for sin with a personal sense of guilt before God is not limited to Old Testament men and women. God requires this same attitude from each person, even today.

Create in me a clean heart, O God,
and renew a steadfast spirit within me.
Psalm 51:10

The apostle Paul encouraged the church in Corinth to live a life of purity — of holiness before God. He told them, "Therefore, having these promises, beloved, let us cleanse ourselves from all filthiness of the flesh and spirit, perfecting holiness in the fear of God" (2 Corinthians 7:1).

He was referring to a previous letter that he had sent them, scolding them about their sinful behavior in the church. Paul rejoiced that they had repented when he wrote in verses 9 and

10, "Now I rejoice, not that you were made sorry, but that your sorrow led to repentance. For you were made sorry in a godly manner, that you might suffer loss from us in nothing. *For godly sorrow produces repentance leading to salvation*, not to be regretted; but the sorrow of the world produces death."

Jesus Himself said, "...Except ye repent ye shall all likewise perish" (Luke 13:3–5 *KJV*). He also said He came to call "sinners to repentance" (Matthew 9:13 *KJV*).

In fact, Jesus appeared to His followers after they had seen him so brutally crucified by the Romans and explained why it all had to happen. The Bible says that Jesus "...opened their understanding, that they might comprehend the Scriptures" (Luke 24:45).

He further explained:

Then He said to them, "Thus it is written, and thus it was necessary for the Christ to suffer and to rise from the dead the third day, and that *repentance* **and** *remission* **of sins should be preached in His name to all nations, beginning at Jerusalem."**

Luke 24:46–47

After Jesus was resurrected from the dead, the apostles continued preaching the gospel, telling the people to "Repent therefore and be converted, that your sins may be blotted out..." (Acts 3:19). That is precisely the message of repentance and remission. "Repentance and remission of sins" are what Jesus told them to declare.

Without this renunciation of sin, we cannot expect forgiveness. *Renounce the works of sin and the lordship of Satan in your life, and confess Jesus as your Lord.*

Believe in Your Heart

Romans 10:9 says if you "*believe* in your heart that God has raised Him from the dead, you will be saved."

When we hear the truth, we must accept it as truth and then act upon that truth.

Our repentance must be mixed with faith in Christ. Many deeply religious people are sorry for their sins, yet they remain in their sins and will die and go to hell for eternity. Why? They stay in their sin because they did not mix that sorrow with faith in the risen Christ who paid the price for their sins.

We must not only believe in "god." We must believe in Jesus Christ and that "God has raised him from the dead...." We must know that Jesus paid the price for our sins. Salvation comes through Christ alone.

The Bible states, "For God so loved the world that He gave His only begotten Son, that whoever believes in Him should not perish but have everlasting life" (John 3:16). This statement is the truth. However, we must accept it as truth if it will be of any benefit to us personally.

Accept the truth of God's Word, not as a general statement about Christ, but as a specific truth *for you*. Today. You must "believe in your heart that God has raised him from the dead."

Salvation comes through Christ alone.
"For God so loved the world that He gave His only
begotten Son, that whoever believes in Him should not
perish but have everlasting life."
John 3:16

This believing is not a mere mental agreement with a religious principle. The Bible says we must believe it in our heart — our inmost, secret place, the very core of our being. It must be accepted without a shadow of doubt within our hearts for it to be real to us.

Faith in Christ Is Not a Mental Exercise

Jesus told His followers in John 5:24, "Most assuredly, I say to you, he who hears My word and believes in Him who sent Me has everlasting life, and shall not come into judgment, but has passed from death into life." Therefore, we must have faith in Christ and no other.

I like what Paul wrote to the Romans about Christ. He said, "But now the righteousness of God apart from the law is revealed, being witnessed by the Law and the Prophets, even the righteousness of God, *through faith in Jesus Christ, to all and on all who believe…*" (Romans 3:21–22).

Our salvation rests upon our faith in the completed work of Jesus Christ.

Confess *Jesus* as Your Lord

Now that we have seen Romans 10:9, let's examine the next verse. "For with the heart one believes unto righteousness, and with the mouth confession is made unto salvation" (Romans 10:10).

---

*Our salvation rests upon our faith
in the completed work of Jesus Christ.*

Something extraordinary happens within us when we believe and accept the truth of God's Word deep within our hearts. When we believe it so much that we are willing to acknowledge the truth, confess our guilt before God and openly confess Jesus as our personal Lord, we are changed by the Spirit of God.

This change is a miraculous work of the Holy Spirit. It is not something we can manufacture with our own efforts. It is not magic, either. It is the wonderful saving grace of the God of eternity who deeply loves us. Jesus said:

> **"If you love Me, keep My commandments. And I will pray the Father, and He will give you another Helper, that He may abide with you forever — the Spirit of truth, whom the world cannot receive, because it neither sees Him nor knows Him; but you know Him, *for He dwells with you and will be in you.* I will not leave you orphans; I will come to you."**
>
> **John 14:15–18**

When we confess Jesus as our Lord, the Holy Spirit comes to live in us. Our spirit becomes alive unto God and is recreated. Now, as a Christian, we can do all things through Christ, who strengthens us because we have the help of His Spirit within.

Something extraordinary happens within us when we believe and accept the truth of God's Word deep within our hearts.

Summary

Therefore, to summarize how you can be born-again:

That if you confess with your mouth the Lord Jesus and believe in your heart that God has raised Him from the dead, you will be saved. For with the heart one believes unto righteousness, and with the mouth confession is made unto salvation.

Romans 10:9–10

Repent and confess Jesus as *your* Lord and Savior, believing that Jesus Christ's death, burial, and resurrection paid for your sins.

You must *say* it aloud with your lips. "Jesus is my Lord."

Repent and confess Jesus as your Lord and Savior, believing that Jesus Christ's death, burial, and resurrection paid for your sins.

Pray the prayer that follows to receive Jesus now.

A Sinner's Prayer
to Receive Jesus as Savior

God in Heaven, I am a sinner. I openly confess to you that I am not living right. I need a Savior.

I believe that Jesus Christ is the Son of God. I believe that Jesus suffered and died for me, taking my sins upon Himself and I believe that You raised Him from the dead.

God, right now, I renounce my former way of life. I turn away from a sinful and selfish life and turn to You, God. I give You my life and make You the Lord of my life from this day forward.

I will live for You from this day until the end of my life. I ask for and receive Your forgiveness and cleansing from sin. I confess that Jesus is now my personal Lord and Savior.

In the name of Jesus, I pray. Amen.

If you prayed that prayer and confessed Jesus as Lord, you will want to mark this day.

Your name: _____

Today's date: _____

CHAPTER 4

BECOMING ESTABLISHED IN FAITH

WHEN YOU WERE BORN AGAIN, you received the life of God in your spirit. God changed you inside, and your spirit is now alive unto God!

Your spirit is the eternal part of you. Your spirit is also where the Spirit of God now lives. Since your spirit is the very core of your being, it is the part of you that will live eternally. Your spirit will continue to exist when you die because you are created in God's image, and He is an eternal Spirit.

However, there is more to you than just your spirit. In his prayer for the church at Thessalonica, Paul prayed, "Now may the God of peace Himself sanctify you completely; and may your whole *spirit, soul, and body* be preserved blameless at the coming of our Lord Jesus Christ" (1 Thessalonians 5:23).

As a newly born-again Christian, you must now begin to care for these three areas of your life: spirit, soul, and body. Doing so will require different types of care for each part of you.

Now may the God of peace Himself sanctify you completely; and may your whole spirit, soul, and body be preserved blameless at the coming of our Lord Jesus Christ.
1 Thessalonians 5:23

We receive the life of God in our spirit, but our mind must be renewed, and our body must be trained and controlled. If they are not, they will do what is natural to them — and they are not the part of us which received salvation from God. They have not yet been changed!

Of course, all three parts — spirit, soul, and body — make a whole. Yet each has a different function as part of the human makeup. We can, however, separate them to study how God created us.

Since Paul gives us their proper order of importance, we should follow his precedent. God's standard of our makeup is the opposite of our worldly upbringing. With God, our spirit comes first. That is clear.

Next on His list is our soul. Since our spirit man is the part of us that touches God, then our soul is the part of us that gives us our human personality. Our soul consists of our mind, will, and emotions.

Last on the list is our body. As important as we know our bodies are, they are of the least importance in the eternal scheme of things. When we die, it is our body that dies. Our body is the shortest-lived part of who we are.

We have our priorities backward, it seems. Without thinking, many Christians use the phrase, "body, soul, and spirit." It sounds religious, but it isn't entirely scriptural.

As a newly born-again Christian,
you must now begin to care for
these three areas of your life: spirit, soul, and body.

The New Testament is an instruction book for believers. It is God's Word to us.

Since the entire New Testament is written to us for instruction in righteousness and our correction, we need to begin reading it daily. From now until we enter heaven, we must spend time each day with God. We must meditate upon what He said through His written Word.

Since it is impossible to cover every instruction given here, I will encapsulate three vital areas for believers.

Keeping Our Spirit Strong

We should do several things consistently to maintain a healthy and strong spirit. If we follow these simple principles, we will grow spiritually.

Notice that I used the word *consistently*! If we have decided to follow the Lord, we must do it wholeheartedly. If we aren't following the Lord with our whole heart, then we have a "false religion," and none of us wants to be a hypocrite.

If we have decided to follow the Lord, we must do it wholeheartedly.

An athlete, for example, must train consistently. If a runner only runs once a week, he will be weak and may even pull a hamstring if he tries to race. No team would take a runner such as that seriously.

Paul wrote to the church at Ephesus, saying, "Finally, my brethren, be strong in the Lord and in the power of His might" (Ephesians 6:10). How then, as a new believer, would one be strong in the Lord?

In that particular passage, Paul explains how to be strong against our spiritual enemy, Satan. In that passage, he urges us to "Put on the whole armor of God, that you may be able to stand against the wiles of the devil" (Ephesians 6:11).

Truth is the first piece of that armor that Paul tells us we'll need to stand against the devil. He instructs, "…having girded your waist with truth…" (Ephesians 6:14). He is writing about the eternal truth of God's Word.

Peter tells us that we were "…born again, not of corruptible seed but incorruptible, through the word of God which lives and abides forever" (1 Peter 1:23). He then quotes the prophet Isaiah who wrote, "But the word of the Lord endures forever" (1 Peter 1:25).

It was the powerful Word of God that was able to transform us into a new creation. His Word is eternal and unchanging, or "incorruptible." It is pure and true. God cannot lie. That is Peter's point, and then he continues instruction for the new believer.

Finally, my brethren, be strong in the Lord
and in the power of His might.
Ephesians 6:10

Therefore, laying aside all malice, all deceit, hypocrisy, envy, and all evil speaking, as newborn babes, *desire the pure milk of the word*, that you may *grow* thereby....

1 Peter 2:1–2

Therefore, the first thing we must do as believers to maintain a strong, healthy spirit and grow up spiritually is to *feed on the Word of God on a consistent basis.*

The best way to pour the Word into our spirit is by reading the Bible daily. The Bible is the inspired Word of God (*see* 2 Peter 1:20–21; 2 Timothy 3:15–17).

The best way to pour the Word into our spirit
is by reading the Bible daily.

This daily Bible reading is where the word *consistency* again comes into play. To become more like God (godly), we must know who God is, how He thinks, and His opinion on the issues of life and death.

Godliness only comes by spending time with God. Allow His Spirit to speak to you as you read His Word. Listen with your heart and not just your intellect. His Word is eternal and is meant to be spiritually understood.

Secondly, we need to receive teaching from Holy Spirit empowered men and women of God — those who are set in the office of pastor by the Lord.

Allow His Spirit to speak to you as you read His Word.

Paul explains that there are certain offices within the Body of Christ. These offices are held by those whom God has chosen and placed in the Body to lead and build up the body of believers.

And He Himself gave some to be apostles, some prophets, some evangelists, and some pastors and teachers, for the equipping of the saints for the work of ministry, for the edifying of the body of Christ.

Ephesians 4:11–12

Every believer, without exception, needs the ministry of these five (or "fivefold") offices. For the new believer, however, pastors are the most important.

All are important and have their function. God placed all five of these offices in the Body of Christ with different gifts and abilities. The evangelist, for instance, is empowered by God to bring unbelievers to a place of decision for Christ. Power and miraculous gifts accompany their ministry.

Yet the body of believers does not need to get saved every Sunday. After we get saved, it is then time to grow into the things of Christ, and that is where our pastor comes into his role in our lives.

Where do you think we will find a pastor preaching and teaching? Primarily in church, where we need to be every week. God gives your pastor an inspired and anointed message, tailor-made by God for your local church. God can speak directly to you through that message; if you are not there, you will not hear it.

I remember going to a supermarket one day where I decided to sit in the café and enjoy a hot dog before shopping. After I went through the line, I sat in a booth and began to eat lunch. Seated across from me were a couple of middle-aged men complaining about their wives. These two were rough-looking characters with calloused hands, camouflaged hunting hats, and well-worn work boots. These two were typical for our region in West Virginia.

At first, I didn't listen to their conversation until one of them mentioned his wife's repeated attempts to get him to attend church with her. She was a church member, and it seemed that she wanted her husband to lead more of a godly example in the family.

As he complained about his wife's attempts, the second fellow began to chime in. He, too, was the victim of his wife's attempts to make him religious. They both built a ponderous case against the church, pastors, Christians, and their own silly, religious wives.

I listened with a mixture of interest and distaste as they built their cases. In the end, they made their final arguments and summation. They agreed, "You don't need to go to church to be a Christian."

This conclusion puzzled me a bit because it seemed that they were claiming to be Christians themselves, though they were acting and speaking with distinctly unchristian verbiage.

While it may be factually accurate that "you don't need to go to church to be a Christian," it is not wise to live that way if you are one. It is also a fact that you will not grow if you are not under the ministry of a pastor. It shows an unsubmissive and rebellious attitude if you are unwilling to allow God's ministry gift to have spiritual authority in your life.

Remember, God places pastors in the Body of Christ for the "...equipping of the saints for the work of ministry, for the edifying of the body of Christ..." (Ephesians 4:12).

Therefore, we need to build our spirits by feeding upon God's Word by spending time reading and meditating upon His Word daily. We need to sit under the ministry of a God-called pastor who loves the people God has put under his care.

Find a church where they believe the Bible is God's Word and the pastor gives his life for the sheep. Then, be there every time the doors are open.

Obey those who rule over you, and be submissive, for they watch out for your souls, as those who must give

account. **Let them do so with joy and not with grief, for that would be unprofitable for you.**

Hebrews 13:17

Not forsaking the assembling of ourselves together, **as is the manner of some, but exhorting one another, and so much the more as you see the Day approaching.**

Hebrews 10:25

Protecting and Renewing our Soul

Our soul — namely our mind, will, and emotions — is distinctly unredeemed. This part of us is unchanged! That is why the Bible tells us what we must do with our soul in numerous passages. It is of the utmost importance, and it is *our* responsibility.

If then you were raised with Christ, *seek those things which are above,* **where Christ is, sitting at the right hand of God. Set your mind on things above, not on things on the earth.**

Colossians 3:1–2

To "seek those things which are above" will take an act of our will. It is our choice, yet God is asking us to do it. He is asking *us* to do it because we are the only ones who can seek the Lord for ourselves. God cannot do that for us.

To "seek those things which are above" will take an act of our will.

More importantly, we see here a principle found throughout the entire Bible. God wants us to serve Him based on our own free will. If we search for Him, we will find Him.

To seek something will take some effort on our part. Seeking is something we do actively and not passively. If you have lost something valuable, you probably turned everything in your house upside down to find it.

We must have this same attitude with eternal things. We must look for, search, and seek for them. If you lost a valuable item, you would hunt for it until you found it.

We Must Change Our Thinking

To "set our minds" upon God and eternal things, we must change our thinking!

In grade school, I learned all the required courses of study. We studied math, English, grammar, geography, science, health, and so on.

Yet my teachers never taught me to discipline my mind beyond listening to the teacher instead of looking out the window. They never had a course entitled, *How to Think Correctly* or *Properly Controlling Your Thought Life*. I could have used a class like that!

To "set our minds" upon God and eternal things, we must change our thinking!

No one ever told me there was a right and wrong way to think, not even in church. Yet God's Word instructs us how to think.

Since we were given eternal life in Christ, we must now focus on things that are eternal. Eternal things are our priority now. Eternal things are essential. If we do not "set our minds on things that are above," we will be consumed with things on the earth. If we seek the cares of this life and the pursuits of pleasure, they will overtake our love for God.

You can readily see the dichotomy. We cannot have it both ways. We are either following the Lord or following our own way. All of this begins with our thinking.

The very next verse in this passage says, "For you died, and your life is hidden with Christ in God" (Colossians 3:3).

Hidden in Christ are all of the blessings of Heaven, and they are ours to enjoy while we live right here on earth. The apostle Paul tells us that we must keep our minds on heavenly things — keep our thoughts on the things of Christ. Our life is in Him, and in Him is the life of God.

As we think about the things of God, we will begin a process the Bible calls "renewing our mind." We must renew our way of thinking.

To renew something means to renovate, refurbish, or repair it. It can also mean to restore, mend, or make good. We need to "renovate, refurbish, or repair" our thinking.

Further down in our Colossians passage, Paul tells us about putting off our former manner of behavior, which catered to the flesh. He writes, "…since you have *put off* the old man with his deeds, and have *put on* the new man who is *renewed* in knowledge according to the image of Him who created him" (Colossians 3:9–10).

Only the Word of God will renew our minds. We will begin to think according to the knowledge that reflects who God is.

If we do not think like God, that is, judge according to what His Word says, we will not act like God; we will act according to what our flesh dictates, just as we always did — as an unregenerate sinner.

An unrenewed mind is why we see so many Christians doing unchristian things. They have not changed their minds according to God's knowledge.

Only the Word of God will renew our minds.

Paul once again wrote about the "new man" in the book of Ephesians. The following passage is significant. God is serious about what we must do.

This I say therefore, and testify in the Lord, that you should no longer walk as the rest of the Gentiles walk, in the *futility of their mind*, having their understanding darkened, being alienated from the life of God, because of the ignorance that is in them, because of the blindness of their heart; who, being past feeling, have given themselves over to lewdness, to work all uncleanness with greediness.

But you have not so learned Christ, if indeed you have heard Him and have been taught by Him, as the truth is in Jesus: that you put off, concerning your former conduct, the old man which grows corrupt according to the deceitful lusts, and be *renewed in the spirit of your mind*, and that you *put on* the new man which was created according to God, in true righteousness and holiness.

Ephesians 4:17–24

Here again, we see where Paul admonishes Christians to "put on" the new man. He refers to the mind, where we wage our battle, in verses 17 and 23.

Summarizing what we have read about what we must do as Christians concerning our souls. We must:

- Seek those things which are above

- Set our minds on things above

- Put off the old man

- Put on the new man

- No longer walk as the rest of the Gentiles walk, in the futility of the mind

- Be renewed in the spirit of your mind

Again, who is responsible for doing these things? Is God going to change our thinking for us? Will God make us "set our minds on things which are above"? Absolutely not! He changed our inner man, and now the rest is left to us.

It is the responsibility of each believer to discipline themselves. We control ourselves by meditating upon God's Word each day and being renewed in our way of thinking.

God will not — indeed, He cannot — do that for us. However, God has given us the most powerful tool in the universe, which is at our disposal daily. That tool is His Word; God's Word is His unchanging, eternal truth.

As Paul was closing his letter to the church in Philippi, he encouraged them with these words:

Finally, brethren, whatever things are true, whatever things are noble, whatever things are just, whatever things are pure, whatever things are lovely, whatever things are of good report, if there is any virtue and if there is anything praiseworthy — meditate on *these* things.

Philippians 4:8

Presenting Our Body to God

We have seen that the Scriptures teach us that we have become a new creation in Christ: "...old things are passed away, behold all things are become new." We are born again.

We have also seen that as born-again believers, we are to begin renewing our minds according to the Word of God and thinking the way the Lord thinks. He wants us to become renewed in the spirit of our mind.

Now we will learn what the Bible tells us to do about our body. In the same way our mind is not made new at the moment of our spiritual rebirth, so it is with our body.

In the twelfth chapter of Romans, Paul instructs Christians on their behavior. He starts by emphatically pleading with us to lead a consecrated and surrendered life to God by saying, "I beseech you therefore, brethren, by the mercies of God, that you *present your bodies a living sacrifice*, holy, acceptable to God, which is your reasonable service" (Romans 12:1).

Because God was merciful to us, He forgave us and cleansed us of sin even though we did not deserve it. Therefore, we could, at the very least, offer our bodies as a holy gift back to the Lord. By doing that, we are worshipping Him for who He is and for what He has done for us. This is the first step in serving God.

This verse also says that your body must be "holy" and "acceptable to God as a living sacrifice." That simply means your body is to be set apart unto God. The word "holy" carries the idea of something very precious and sacred.

When you consider and regard your body as holy or set apart and very precious because of the price paid for it and for you as a whole person, presenting it as "a living sacrifice" is the very minimum thing you can do for God. It is "your reasonable service."

It is almost a contradiction. Our body is not yet redeemed and continues to desire all sinful things for which it has always lusted. In contrast, even though it is corrupt and against our spirit, we must deem it holy and set apart! Our bodies are precious property — bought and paid for by the Blood of Jesus.

We would not be serving the purposes and plans of God if we were to do whatever we felt like doing; just because we *can* does not mean that we *should*. Doing whatever our flesh feels like will defeat us in every other area of life. The apostle Peter wrote, "Beloved, I beg you as sojourners and pilgrims, abstain from fleshly lusts *which war against the soul*" (1 Peter 2:11).

If you haven't already, you will soon notice that your flesh will put up a fight with you. That is because what your flesh wants is opposed to what your spirit wants. Paul wrote, "Therefore, put to death your members which are on the earth: fornication, uncleanness, passion, evil desire, and covetousness, which is idolatry" (Colossians 3:5). This is only a partial list of vices, but they illustrate the point.

Our bodies are precious property — bought and paid for by the Blood of Jesus.

For example, if a person is *covetous,* they are *greedy.* Greed is an idol in that a greedy person puts the acquisition and possession of material things before their desire to serve the Lord. Many Christian people have refused to give the tithe because of greed in their hearts. That greed wars against your soul! Your inner man wants to serve God with what He has given you, but your flesh wants to consume all things upon itself, and your unrenewed mind thinks it is losing something by giving it to God. We cannot serve two masters.

The rest of Colossians chapter three tells us of the benefit of putting on the new man and God's wrath coming upon those who are disobedient to Him. It also lists a few more vices, which makes clear God's opinion on the subject.

As a new believer in Christ, you must learn to walk in the spirit. That will be something totally new. However, walking in the spirit is vital, and there are good reasons why God tells you to do it.

Paul wrote, "I say then: Walk in the Spirit, and you shall not fulfill the lust of the flesh" (Galatians 5:16). "The flesh" obviously refers to our body.

If we concentrate on one action, "walk in the Spirit," we will not do the other, "fulfill the lust of the flesh" — that is, we will not gratify our flesh and the desires of our body.

Many say, "I could never become a Christian because I can't live that kind of lifestyle." But thank God, He has given us a way to be victorious in every area in which He has commanded us to be obedient.

He gave us His Word so we can think as He does. He gave us His Spirit so we can behave as Jesus did, without sinning in the body. God gave us the tools to be successful in this life.

God gave us the tools to be successful in this life.

Held Captive

Although some may say it is unrealistic or even unfair for God to require His people to live according to godly standards, we must realize that everything He commands us to do is for our own benefit.

Many will say God takes all the fun out of life by requiring Christians not to walk in sin. That attitude is a prime example of the need for a renewed way of thinking!

Even though sinners assume that they are living life to the fullest by sinning, they do not realize they are held captive by the sin they commit. Paul wrote, "Knowing this, that our old man was crucified with Him, that the body of sin might be done away with, that we should no longer be *slaves of sin*" (Romans 6:6).

That is a power-packed verse! If you read the entire sixth chapter of Romans, you will see that Jesus completely freed us from sin. Being free from sin is better than being enslaved to our passions and lusts. When you are a slave, you must do whatever your master tells you. As a slave to sin, you must do whatever sin tells you. There is no choice but to sin because it owns you!

It is to our advantage not to be enslaved. It is for our benefit that Christ has set us free from it.

There is no denying the fact that there are pleasures in sinning. That is the reason we do it! Yet that pleasure and fun will wear out and become less and less satisfying, leading us into a more profound need to increase that sin to gain the satisfaction we once got from it initially.

The more we sin, the deeper we become enslaved to it. We will obey its commands without thinking.

That is why Paul commands us to "...put to death your members which are on the earth..." (Colossians 3:5). He also admonishes that "...our old man was crucified with Him, that the body of sin might be done away with..." (Romans 6:6).

Paul goes on to write, "Likewise reckon ye also yourselves to be dead indeed unto sin, but alive unto God through Jesus Christ our Lord. *Let not sin therefore reign in your mortal body, that ye should obey it in the lusts thereof*" (Romans 6:11–12 *KJV*).

Even with the best intentions in mind, if we keep sin alive in our hearts, we will eventually act upon it. That is why the Bible teaches us to "reckon ourselves to be dead" unto sin. That means we are to consider, deem, surmise, and think of ourselves as dead to sin. Think of it this way; if you are dead to something, you can no longer feel it. A dead man can feel nothing and will not respond to anything. He is dead!

This analogy is for us. Not only do we consider ourselves inactive and deadened to the flesh's sinful desires, but we have also been given the great gift of a replacement for that sin. God doesn't simply take something away from us. He gave us Christ in its stead. We are not only dead to sin; we are now "alive unto God through Jesus Christ our Lord" (Romans 6:11). Paul explains:

> **And do not present your members as instruments of unrighteousness to sin, but present yourselves to God as being alive from the dead, and your members as instruments of righteousness to God. For sin shall not have dominion over you, for you are not under Law but under grace.**
>
> **Romans 6:13–14**

The choice is a part of our repentance. It is part of the whole package. We are the only ones who can present our members.

When we repent and ask Christ to be our Lord, we receive remission of our sins and the free gift of eternal life. Jesus paid the full price for us to have all that. However, if we expect to pray a little prayer, asking God to forgive us without true repentance — with works that correspond to it — we are not being honest. We would be asking God for something without any commitment in return. We cannot expect to receive forgiveness of sins if we plan to regard iniquity in our hearts and continue to walk in darkness.

I strongly urge you to take time today and read the sixth chapter of Romans. The book of Romans is Paul's premier work of New Testament theology. In the letter to the Romans, Paul explains the transition from the Old Testament obligation of the Law to the personal freedom of each believer from sin in the New Testament.

The remainder of chapter six speaks of being "free from sin" repeatedly. That is our position in Christ. Why should we continue in the turmoil of slavery to the passions and lusts of our flesh and minds? We must now yield ourselves to the freedom purchased for us through the shed Blood of Christ and "walk in newness of life."

Therefore we were buried with Him through baptism into death, that just as Christ was raised from the dead by the glory of the Father, even so we also should walk in newness of life.

Romans 6:4

CHAPTER 5

LET'S SUM IT UP

To summarize, let me say this — God has provided a way for all lost mankind to return to Himself.

Man is a sinful being from birth and cannot save himself. Man's problem is sin. God solved that problem through His Son, Jesus Christ.

God has provided a way for all lost mankind to return to Himself.

There is only one God and only one way to reach God.

Jesus said we must be born again. Believing that He is Lord and that His sacrifice is sufficient to free us from sin is the way to salvation. We must decide. Will we believe, repent, and confess Jesus as our Lord?

When we make Jesus our Lord, God changes us in our inner man — our spirit.

Jesus said we must be born again.

If we are born again, there will be evidence. That evidence will be the fruit of our lives. We can see from our fruit that there is a change in our inner man. It isn't necessary to judge someone's heart, for only God sees the heart. However, a person's fruit tells the story. That fruit is outward for all to see.

If there is no godly fruit, there is no change.

In the third chapter, I discussed how to become a born-again person, as Jesus requires. If you need to review that and meditate on what God says, it will build faith in your heart to hear the Word of God on the subject. He will give you the faith to receive His free gift.

After we become a child of God, we must begin the lifelong process of becoming like Him in every aspect of our being. That takes time, and it is a process. We must continually be growing.

If you're a new believer, you should seek out a church that believes the Bible is God's inspired Word to the world. Find a church where the pastor is called by God to care for the church members, as a shepherd cares for his sheep. A pastor with a pastor's heart is someone that you need. Choose to give that pastor spiritual authority in your life.

The pastor's job is to care for your soul. They do not have the authority to tell you what color car to buy or where to live, but they do have the authority to teach you the Word of God and have spiritual oversight. They can also help us get back on the right path when we slip up.

God doesn't expect us to be perfect. He does, however, expect us to walk by faith and become mature believers.

I pray that you may increase in all things and become more like Him. He is worthy to be praised.

CHAPTER 6

MY FINAL THOUGHTS

THERE ARE MANY THINGS THAT you should do as a Christian person. However, the most important things are of the heart.

Jesus quoted the Law from the book of Deuteronomy 6:5, "You shall love the LORD your God with all your heart, with all your soul, and with all your strength." That is what God has always wanted from us since creation.

God put such a high premium on it that He continued on to command the Israelites that they must keep these words in their hearts and should teach the words that He commanded them that day to their children. Love God, and love His Word.

Today, under New Testament instructions, we are no longer required to do things from obligation. Today, we have the Holy Spirit living inside of us to guide us and help us live a right life.

However, if we try to live as a spiritual Christian without revering and obeying the Word of God in our hearts, just the way God commanded the Israelites, we are deceiving ourselves.

Love God, and love His Word.

Deuteronomy 6:6 says, "And these words which I command you today shall be in your heart." In short, we must value the Word of God above all else to be like Christ.

Jesus spoke to the issue of our heart by teaching the teachers of the Law the greatest commandment. Since we are no longer obligated to obey every commandment in the Law of Moses, what are we supposed to do to be right and holy? We have to have the Law of God written in our heart, and our actions should show it.

The Greatest Commandment

But when the Pharisees heard that He had silenced the Sadducees, they gathered together. Then one of them, a lawyer, asked Him a question, testing Him, and saying, "Teacher, which is the great commandment in the law?"

Jesus said to him, "'You shall love the LORD your God with all your heart, with all your soul, and with all your mind.' This is the first and great commandment. And the second is like it: 'You shall love your neighbor as yourself.' On these two commandments hang all the Law and the Prophets."

Matthew 22:34–40

This lawyer was insincere in asking Jesus what the greatest commandment was. The verse said he was "testing Him" (Matthew 22:35). He was trying to trick Jesus and trip Him up, so to speak, because He had "silenced the Sadducees."

To this point, Jesus said there were two commandments in the Law that we should follow. Jesus said, "'You shall love the LORD your God with all your heart, with all your soul, and with all your mind.' This is the first and great commandment" (Matthew 22:37–38).

According to Jesus, that was the most essential Law, the "first and great commandment."

The second in importance is like it: "You shall love your neighbor as yourself" (Matthew 22:39).

Why were those so important? Matthew 22:40 says, "On these two commandments hang all the Law and the Prophets." I believe Jesus tells us that we can now fulfill the Law by walking in love. Love is the Law of the New Testament. With the Holy Spirit living inside of each believer, we can walk in love, which is far beyond what you and I can do as a person without the Spirit of God.

James' Instructions to Gentile Believers

After a great controversy during the transition from the obligation to the Law of Moses to the New Testament, the church in Antioch of Syria sent the apostle Paul to Jerusalem to deal with the issue of "circumcision," or obeying the Law to be a Christian.

Acts 15:1 gives us the context of the controversy: "And certain men came down from Judea and taught the brethren, 'Unless you are circumcised according to the custom of Moses, you cannot be saved.'"

This was during the first century when the Church was just developing. Paul, the apostle, had been called by God and trained by the Spirit. He had been preaching to the gentiles and had already gone on a missionary journey, which almost cost him his very life.

Paul became the leading apostle to those who had not been part of the Jewish religious system, those not born as Jews or Hebrews. Jesus died for all.

The believers in Antioch of Syria, where Paul was a leader, decided to send him and Barnabas to Jerusalem to sort out an issue to which they did not have an answer. There was great dissension (argument) about circumcision because many Jewish leaders from Jerusalem, who had become believers in Jesus, were teaching false doctrine.

Jesus died for all.

Therefore, when Paul and Barnabas had no small *dissension* and *dispute* with them, they determined that Paul and Barnabas and certain others of them should go up to Jerusalem, to the apostles and elders, about this question.

Acts 15:2

I would strongly suggest that you read Acts 15 for the whole story. I cannot cover it in its entirety here.

The Church needed a final ruling on this matter, so they held a council in Jerusalem. The twelve apostles and the elders came together there to hear arguments. It says that "when there had been much dispute, Peter rose up and said..." (Acts 15:7).

Peter, who had become the most revered of the original apostles, lent his experience with the conversion and miracles he had experienced among the gentiles. He knew that it was God's will to save them. Peter said, "and made no distinction between us and them, purifying their hearts by faith" (Acts 15:9).

Peter's words resounded among the Jews when he said, "Now therefore, why do you test God by putting a yoke on the neck of the disciples which neither our fathers nor we were able to bear?" (Acts 15:10).

Therefore, when Peter rose to speak about what God had done through his ministry, the whole crowd was silent and then listened to Paul and Barnabas (*see* Acts 15:12).

My point is that James, pastor of the church in Jerusalem where the converted Jews attended, concluded that the new disciples in Antioch, Syria, and Cilicia did not have to obey the law of Moses to be true Christians (*see* Acts 15:13–29).

He wrote a letter to be read to all the churches of the gentiles that they merely needed to stop acting like pagans and serve God.

I love the words James wrote to them: "For it seemed good to the Holy Spirit, and to us, to lay upon you no greater burden than these necessary things" (Acts 15:28). Then, the following verse lists the pagan practices they were involved in before they believed. "If you keep yourselves from these, you will do well" (Acts 15:29).

In conclusion, be born again, be filled with the Holy Spirit, love God, value His Word, and write it upon your heart. Do so, and you will do well.

My Final Thoughts

www.ingramcontent.com/pod-product-compliance
Lightning Source LLC
Chambersburg PA
CBHW020338130626
46549CB00003B/1206